If I Were a Penguin

By Meg Gaertner

level 2
little blue readers

www.littlebluehousebooks.com

Little Blue House is distributed by North Star Editions:
sales@northstareditions.com | 888-417-0195

Produced for Little Blue House by Red Line Editorial.

Photographs ©: iStockphoto, cover, 4, 6–7, 9, 10, 16, 18–19, 21, 23, 24 (top left), 24 (top right), 24 (bottom left); Shutterstock Images, 13, 14–15, 24 (bottom right)

Library of Congress Control Number: 2020913849

ISBN
978-1-64619-304-2 (hardcover)
978-1-64619-322-6 (paperback)
978-1-64619-358-5 (ebook pdf)
978-1-64619-340-0 (hosted ebook)

Printed in the United States of America
Mankato, MN
012021

About the Author

Meg Gaertner enjoys reading, writing, dancing, and being outside. She thinks the way penguins move on land is funny. She lives in Minnesota.

Table of Contents

If I Were a Penguin

I would be a bird.

But I would not be able

to fly.

I would have flippers instead of wings. My flippers would help me swim.

I would spend some
of my time on land.
I would spend some
of my time in the ocean.

Food and Safety

My back would be black, and my front would be white.

My colors would help me stay safe in the ocean. They would help me hide from seals.

I would catch my food in the ocean.

I would eat mostly fish.

colony

Life in a Colony

I would live in a colony.

A colony is a group

of penguins.

I would stand close
to other penguins.
We would keep one
another warm.

I would have one or two eggs, and I would keep them warm.

egg

I would feed my chick,
and I would keep it safe.

Glossary

chick

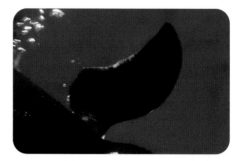

flipper

colony

seal

Index